W9-AAS-747

CHINA
the people

Bobbie Kalman

A Bobbie Kalman Book
The Lands, Peoples, and Cultures Series

Crabtree Publishing Company

j951
KAL

The Lands, Peoples, and Cultures Series

Created by Bobbie Kalman

For my cousins Paula and Christina

Written by
Bobbie Kalman

Coordinating editor
Ellen Rodger

Editor
Jane Lewis

Contributing editor
Lisa Gurusinghe

Editors/first edition
Janine Schaub
Christine Arthurs
Margaret Hoogeveen

Production coordinator
Rose Gowsell

Production
Arlene Arch

Separations and film
Embassy Graphics

Printer
Worzalla Publishing Company

Illustrations
Dianne Eastman: icons
David Wysotski, Allure Illustrations: back cover

Photographs
Jim Bryant: p. 6 (lower left), 13 (bottom), 16 (left), 21 (bottom); Joan Lebold Cohen/Photo Researchers: p. 5 (bottom); courtesy of the Consulate General of the People's Republic of China: p. 6 (top & bottom right); Dennis Cox/ChinaStock: p. 8, 10, 11 (right), 15 (top left), 17 (top), 18 (left), 23 (top), 25 (bottom), 29 (top left); Peter Crabtree: p. 23 (bottom); Betty Crowell: p. 1, 16 (right); Judie Davies: p. 7; Tim Davis/Photo Researchers: p. 25 (top); Ken Ginn: p. 13 (top), 26; George Holton/Photo Researchers: p. 20 (bottom); Wolfgang Kaehler: p. 4 (bottom), 5 (top), 14, 15 (top right), 19 (top left, bottom), 20 (top), 24, 27 (bottom), 28 (both), 29 (top right, bottom), 31 (top left); Liu Liqun/ChinaStock: p. 12, 19 (top right); Christopher Liu/ChinaStock: p. 11 (left), 15 (bottom), 18 (right), 27 (top), 31 (bottom); Ruth Malloy: p. 22; Zhao Meichang: p. 21 (top); Pat Morrow/First Light: p. 9, 31 (top right); Larry Rossignol: p. 6 (top left); Liu Xiaoyang/ChinaStock: p. 4 (top); other images by Digital Stock

Every effort has been made to obtain the appropriate credit and full copyright clearance for all images in this book. Any oversights or omissions will be corrected in future editions.

Cover: A young woman from Inner Mongolia in traditional Mongolian dress.

Title page: A group of children gather in front of the lense of a passing photographer.

Back cover: The Giant Panda lives in the bamboo forests and mountain regions of southwestern China.

Published by
Crabtree Publishing Company

PMB 16A
350 Fifth Avenue
Suite 3308
New York
N.Y. 10118

612 Welland Avenue
St. Catharines
Ontario, Canada
L2M 5V6

73 Lime Walk
Headington
Oxford OX3 7AD
United Kingdom

Copyright © **2001 CRABTREE PUBLISHING COMPANY**. All rights reserved. No part of this publication may be reproduced, stored in a retrieval system or be transmitted in any form or by any means, electronic, mechanical, photocopying, recording, or otherwise, without the prior written permission of Crabtree Publishing Company.

Cataloging in Publication Data

Kalman, Bobbie
China, the people / Bobbie Kalman. – Rev. ed.
p.cm – (The lands, peoples, and cultures series)
Includes index.
ISBN 0-7787-9379-6 (RLB) – ISBN 0-7787-9747-3 (pbk.)
1. China–Social conditions–1976–Juvenile literature.
[1. China–Social life and customs.] I. Title. II Series.
HN733.5 .K3 2001
306'.0951–dc21
00-057081
LC

Contents

One billion strong

There are over one billion people living in China today. That is more than one-sixth of the people on Earth! During the past 4,000 years, the Chinese people have experienced many changes in their country. Their **ancestors** lived through times of war, famine, flood, and several different systems of government. Out of this complicated history, the Chinese people have emerged with a rich **culture** and a strong spirit.

Farming, industry, and trade have increased in China over the last twenty years. Many Chinese people are incorporating modern elements into their traditional lifestyle. Hobbies and cultural activities such as **martial arts** and festivals are a part of Chinese life. Many Chinese people are also enjoying an expanding Chinese economy and greater access to consumer goods.

Hoping for a better future

Although many aspects of life in China have improved, the Chinese people have little say in the decisions made by their government. In June 1989, thousands of students and other concerned citizens staged protests in Tiananmen Square. They wanted to bring about changes in the government. The government sent in troops armed with guns. Hundreds of people were killed and many others were imprisoned. Since then, China has made many changes to its economic system but few changes to its government. All changes are being made slowly. Someday, people all over China hope to own property and earn and spend money with fewer restrictions.

The people shown on these pages represent the various cultural groups of China. They come from different backgrounds, speak different languages, and practice different religions.

5

Chinese people do not share a common background and lifestyle. China is a mixture of dozens of **national groups** whose beliefs and customs vary. One of China's challenges is to unite all its peoples even though they may live far apart and speak many different languages.

The Han majority

There are fifty-six national groups in China. These groups have lived in China for thousands of years. The majority of the population is Han Chinese. The Han trace their ancestry to the Han Dynasty, which ruled China for 400 years during ancient times. They are bound together by a culture that is over 2,000 years old. They originally lived in the eastern river basins, but over hundreds of years have migrated all over China.

Non-Han groups

The fifty-five other national groups of China make up eight percent of the present population. Eight percent may seem like a small number, but it is over one hundred million people! The non-Han nationalities are considered **minority** groups because they are greatly outnumbered by the Han Chinese. Each group has a unique culture.

Autonomous regions

China is divided into twenty-one provinces and five **autonomous**, or independent, regions. An autonomous region is an area where many people from one minority group live. Although these areas are controlled by the Chinese government, their inhabitants are allowed to follow some of their traditional ways. Dozens of smaller autonomous counties can also be found within areas where Han Chinese live. These are home to several minority groups, such as the Miao, Bouyei, and Bai. Some autonomous regions did not become part of China by choice. Many people in these areas want their nations to be independent again so they can govern themselves and follow their own cultural lifestyles.

The five autonomous regions are Tibet, Xinjiang, Inner Mongolia, Ningxia, and Guangxi. Except for Guangxi, which is in China's mid-south, these regions are near the borders of China. Harsh climates and rugged landscapes have caused the people who live in these regions— the Uygurs, Kazaks, Kirgiz, Tibetans, Mongols, and Hui—to live in small, scattered communities.

Miao and Bouyei artisans

Many Miao counties are scattered throughout Guizhou province. The Miao live in unique hanging houses and wear delicately embroidered, homespun clothing. Miao artisans are well known for their silversmithing techniques and finely crafted pottery. The Bouyei, like the Miao, also live in Guizhou province. They are famous for their blue-and-white carpets.

(opposite page, clockwise from top left) A Bai woman carries her child in a backpack.

Bouyei women embroider their hand-woven clothes with flowers and symbols of long life.

On special occasions, Miao women wear headdresses and large silver ornaments all over their clothes.

Bai headdresses have fringes. Single women wear long tassels; married women wear short ones.

(below) An elderly Han Chinese man.

Tibet is an isolated area. It is sometimes called "the roof of the world" because its average height above sea level is 13,124 feet (4000 m).

The Bai

The Bai have lived in China's interior for over a thousand years. Today, around one million Bai live in autonomous areas within Yunnan Province. Many work in marble quarries, as their ancestors did before them, lugging huge pieces of stone on their backs. Local Bai sculptors use some of the marble to create vases and other ornaments; the rest is shipped to far-off places to be used in the construction of buildings. When Bai villagers are constructing a building, they have a celebration after the roof beam has been raised. They throw coins baked in bread from the roof to ensure wealth. This celebration is part of Bai **folk religion**.

The Tibetans

The **plateau** of Tibet is located in southwest China, to the north of the Himalayan mountains. The Tibetans who live there depend on farming and animal herding for survival. They grow barley and keep large, shaggy, animals called yaks, which supply them with meat and dairy products. Tibetans practice an ancient religion known as **Lama Buddhism** which is based on the teachings of Buddha and the Dalai Lama.

Life in the desert

The Uygurs, Kazaks, and Kirgiz live in areas across the northwest of China in the autonomous region of Xinjiang and throughout desert provinces such as Gansu. These groups continue to live as they have for centuries, depending on farming and herding for their livelihood. Gravel covers the dry, hard ground of the Xinjiang region. The people who live there must endure extremely cold winters and hot summers. Sometimes the temperature climbs higher than 104°F (40°C); at other times it drops below -40°F (-40°C). Sudden dust storms are common, and thick clouds of sand can blot out the sun completely. Farming is difficult because there is little soil that is suitable for planting crops. Crops can be grown only in the moist ground near an **oasis**. An oasis is an isolated area of land in the desert kept fertile by a series of underground springs. Turpan, an oasis north of the Taklimakan Desert, is the hottest and lowest spot in China. It is almost 656 feet (200 m) below sea level.

Homes of the sun-baked clay

The Uygurs are farmers who live in adobe houses. Adobe is a type of brick made from sun-baked clay. Adobe homes have deep cellars that stay cool even when it is extremely hot outside. The Uygur diet consists mainly of lamb, rice, and fruit grown in the oases. Uygur women wear flowered skirts, dark stockings, and embroidered skull caps on their heads. The men also wear caps, along with knee-high boots and two-piece suits. The Uygurs follow the religion of **Islam**.

Living in *yurts*

Like the Uygurs, the Kazaks and Kirgiz follow the Islamic faith, but their lifestyles are much different. The Kazaks and Kirgiz are tent-dwelling **nomads**. Nomads are people who frequently move from place to place looking for food and land on which their animals can graze.

The Kazaks herd sheep and goats, and the Kirgiz herd yaks, goats, camel, sheep, and horses. The houses of the Kazaks and Kirgiz are dome-shaped tents called *yurts*. A *yurt* consists of many layers of felt laid over a portable wooden frame and tied down with ropes. When it is time to move, the entire structure can be folded up into a bundle and moved to another location.

The Mongols

The autonomous region of Inner Mongolia is located in the north. Six hundred years ago, the Mongol people were the rulers of China. They came from Mongolia and started the Yuan Dynasty. After the Ming Dynasty took power, the Mongols settled in their current location—below the Mongolian border, next to the Gobi Desert. Like the Kazaks and Kirgiz, the Mongols have led nomadic lives for centuries. They, too, live in *yurts* and herd sheep and camels on horseback.

Around 100,000 Kirgiz inhabit China's far west. As nomads, Kirgiz carry only a few belongings, so their colorful, hand-woven wall hangings and rugs are used for many purposes.

Family life

The **extended family** has been a traditional part of Chinese society for many years. Extended families include family members such as aunts, uncles, cousins, and grandparents. In the past, Chinese homes were crowded because several **generations** lived together under one roof, and couples usually had many children. Villages were made up of several farming families that were often related to one another. Living in a Chinese village was like being at a big family reunion every day!

Enduring relationships

Today, Chinese couples have fewer children and more people live in cities, but the extended family is still a part of life in China. Most village families work together on farms or in factories. Elderly Chinese people usually live with their married children and grandchildren, especially in rural areas. In cities, it is common for three generations of a family to live together in one building because there are not enough homes for everyone.

Respect for elders

Older people have an important place in Chinese society. They are respected for their knowledge and experience. Their advice is sought and carefully considered in family decisions. Chinese grandmothers receive special treatment because they are considered to be the heads of households. Chinese people feel it is their duty to care for their elderly parents. Some cities provide "Homes of Respect for the Aged" for those who do not have an extended family to look after them.

(above) This father and daughter are out for lunch in a park.

(left) In rural areas, most people work with their children alongside them. In cities, the state provides day care.

Links with the past

The Chinese respect their elders and keep the memories of their ancestors alive. They believe that every person, living or dead, is a link in a long chain of people that stretches back to ancient times. Even though ancestors are dead, living relatives still feel that they influence daily life.

The changing family

The Chinese family has changed in many ways in the last one hundred years. In the old days, men and women did not choose their own marriage partners. Matchmakers brought them together. This practice is now illegal, although some marriages are still arranged in rural areas. Today most couples marry for love. To prevent large families, which cause China's already immense population to increase, the government discourages people from marrying until they are in their mid-twenties.

Family jobs

In China, everyone has family responsibilities. When grandparents retire from working, they often take care of their grandchildren and do much of the shopping and cooking. These are helpful tasks because in many young Chinese families, both parents work outside the home.

As well as having jobs, adults belong to committees that help run their neighborhoods. Even the children contribute in some way. Village children may have to feed the chickens or look after their younger brothers or sisters. City children spend time doing community work, such as cleaning classrooms or streets.

Separated families

In some families, one of the marriage partners is required to take a government-assigned job in a faraway city. This enforced separation sometimes puts a lot of stress on family relationships.

11

One-child families

In the past, most Chinese citizens had large families with a lot of children. Children had many chores, such as helping look after the farm animals. With several children, parents could be assured of being cared for in their old age. Even though there were many births every year, China's population stayed about the same because many people died due to disease or starvation. Today, however, there are better **sanitary conditions**, medical services, and food supplies. Fewer babies die, and people live longer than ever. This has caused the population to increase at a rapid rate. Every year, China grows by seventeen million people!

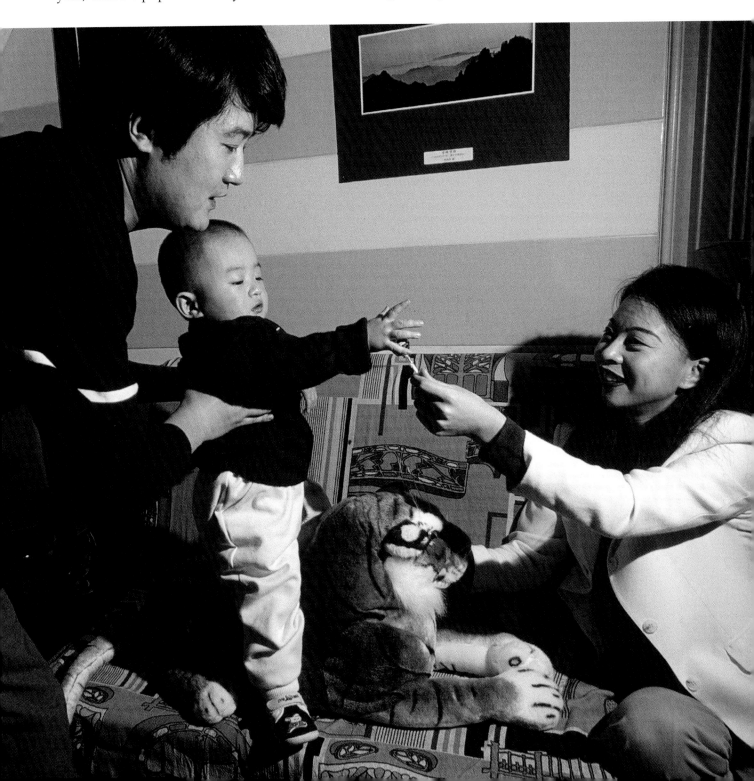

One-child rewards

In order to control the growth of the population, the Chinese government has tried to convince couples to have only one child. The one-child policy has been in effect since the 1970s. Couples that have only one child are given a yearly bonus and certain other privileges. They receive assistance in finding housing, and visits to the doctor or hospital are paid for by the government. The child is placed at the top of the list for a spot in kindergarten or primary school. This is an advantage because there is a shortage of teachers and classroom space in China.

Serious measures

Families that have more than one child are punished. The government withdraws the yearly bonus, charges the parents a fine, and gives the family fewer privileges. A family that has a third child receives even harsher penalties. The parents may lose their jobs and the family must pay all its medical expenses.

The Chinese government has made a remarkable effort to control its population growth, but the program has not turned out to be a complete success. Controlling population is a difficult task. People do not like being told not to have children. Many people want families so badly that they are willing to pay fines and suffer the other penalties for having more than one child.

Exceptions to the rule

Some changes have been made in the one-child policy. A city couple may now have a second child if their first child is a girl. In traditional Chinese culture, it is seen as important to have a boy. Boys are expected to support and take care of their parents when they grow old. The one-child policy is most strictly enforced in the cities. Families living in rural areas no longer have to follow the policy. The rural areas of China are less crowded, and larger families can live more comfortably. As well, children are needed to help out with the farm work or family business. Minority groups are also allowed to have more than one child.

The ancient Chinese saying, "Children are as precious as jade," is more true today than ever before. The children of one-child families enjoy special attention from their parents and privileges from the state.

Clothing

Chinese people wear western-style clothing such as pants, skirts, and shirts as well as traditional Chinese clothing. In warm areas, people stay cool by wearing clothes made of natural fabrics such as silk and cotton. In colder regions, people wear quilted fabrics and fur-lined coats and hats.

Clothing colors

Historically, the color of clothing told a great deal about social status. Emperors wore yellow, which symbolised wealth and power. They also wore bright colors such as green, black, and red. Today, red and gold symbolise happiness and good fortune, and white symbolises wealth.

The Mao suit

Many Chinese people wear a jacket and pants known as a Mao suit. The Mao suit was created by Mao Zedong as clothing for people in the military. Eventually, all Chinese people began wearing the heavy jacket and pants. These clothes were durable and warm, which was necessary during times when many Chinese people could not afford to buy new clothes. Today, the Mao suit is still a common sight on the streets of most Chinese towns and cities.

(above) Millions of Chinese people wear Mao shirts and trousers — even little children!

(above) These colorfully dressed Li women are from Hainan Island.

(right) This Hua Yao Dai woman from Yunnan Province is in traditional dress.

(below) Buyi women from Guizhou.

Many kinds of homes

Chinese homes are built to suit the various landscapes and weather conditions of China. To shelter them from the wind, some houses are built beside mountains. Others are built with deep cellars to keep them cool. Many houses in flood-prone areas stand on strong stilts. These designs suit the regions in which the homes are built, and they also reflect the cultures of the people who live in them.

Traditional houses

Older houses in China are one story high with whitewashed walls. Their upswept roofs are made of overlapping dark-blue tiles. Support beams are often intricately carved with ancient symbols. Most houses consist of two large rooms, plus a kitchen, and a bathroom. Courtyards make up for these tight living quarters. Several houses join onto one courtyard, where trickling fountains and moist plants help bring down the temperature during hot weather. Families and neighbors play games and eat outside in this pleasant atmosphere. Wooden gates separate the courtyard from the busy streets.

Different living conditions

Fresh running water is a luxury that people in some countries take for granted. Many Chinese homes do not have indoor taps or flush toilets. Instead, the Chinese get their water from outdoor taps or neighborhood wells. It is still common to see people in rural areas carrying home their daily supply of water in wooden buckets hanging from a bamboo pole across their shoulders. Electricity is precious in China. Most city homes have electricity, but many families use it only sparingly. Central heating in village homes is rare. People wear several layers of padded jackets and trousers if their houses are too cold.

(left) In rocky areas, dwellings known as hanging houses are built right onto cliffsides.

(below) Many Chinese families work and live aboard houseboats called sampans.

Concrete communities

Many people in China's cities live in concrete apartment buildings. In some areas, groups of these buildings are built close together to form apartment complexes with shops and schools. The individual apartments are small. Some families have to share a kitchen and bathroom. Rent is inexpensive because these homes are provided by the government. Some people are making extra money under the government's new policies and eventually buy their own homes.

A cave called home

Millions of people in northern China live in cavelike dwellings that are practical and comfortable. These homes stay warm in winter and cool in summer. Some cave houses are dug out of hill-sides. This allows people to use the flat land of the hilltops and valleys for farming. The most interesting cave homes are built below ground level. First, a huge pit is dug into the ground. Then houses are carved out of the sides of the pit, and the pit becomes a courtyard. Some cave homes have bricked-in fronts with glass windows.

(top) A small number of people in China live in large, comfortable homes with beautiful gardens.

(inset) Thousands of people live in apartment buildings in China's crowded cities.

Living on the water

Thousands of Chinese people live and work right on the water. They live on *sampans*, which are small cargo boats that cruise up and down China's main rivers. These people make their living by shipping goods to and from river ports. Most of them rarely have to come ashore. Instead of attending regular school, children who live on *sampans* are taught by traveling tutors.

 # City life

China is changing rapidly as it races to become a modern **industrialized** nation. These changes are having tremendous effects on living conditions in both the city and country. Let's take a look at how the daily lives of the Chinese are affected by some of these changes.

Growing cities

About three hundred million people live in China's cities. Older cities that have been highly populated for a long time are now even more crowded. New cities are growing up along the rivers and wherever business is booming.

Modern conveniences

People who live in China's cities enjoy a higher standard of living than those who live in villages. Cities provide people with a wider variety of goods and services. Although living conditions are cramped, most homes have central heating, electricity, and gas stoves. Many city people earn enough money to buy television sets and fashionable clothes. They also have more free time to pursue leisure activities and hobbies. City living does have its problems, however. Large cities, especially Beijing, Shanghai, and Chongqing, are crowded and polluted.

(left) People who live in cities such as Shanghai have access to electricity, public transportation, and better health care.

(below) Thousands of people are employed in China's growing business sector.

(above) Large supermarkets provide city dwellers with a wide range of products.

(left) The demand for western goods is growing, and businesses such as McDonald's® are opening their doors in China.

(below) Old and new ways blend on China's city streets.

Village life

People who live in rural China work hard and lead busy and difficult lives. Families often do all the field work **manually** because farming equipment is rare and expensive. All kinds of construction, from building roads to digging sewers, are completed by hand. Many villagers take on second jobs in factories when there is not enough work to make a living on their farms.

Lack of services

Remote villages have few of the advantages of modern society. Running water and electricity are rare. These services are in great demand, but it will take a long time before they are set up. Shortages of goods also occur in rural areas.

(right) Many rural children grow up to be farmers like their parents.

(below) In this remote village, a Kazak woman uses a hand-operated sewing machine to make clothing.

(left) A young girl operates a raft that is used to ferry villagers across the river.

(below) Villagers continue to wash their clothes by hand. Many rural areas are still without modern conveniences.

Language and communication

Chinese is an ancient language that is extremely difficult to master. A North American person learning Chinese might think that two words sound exactly the same, but the words actually have different meanings depending on the tone in which they are spoken. *Fu*, for example, means both "happiness" and "bat," depending on the pitch of the speaker's voice.

A natural voice

China is a huge country and its people speak many different **dialects**. A dialect is a regional variety of a language with its own vocabulary and pronunciation. The Chinese from one region often find it impossible to communicate with the Chinese from another region. In order to solve this problem, the Chinese government declared the Mandarin dialect, or *putonghua*, to be the national language. A massive campaign was launched forty years ago to teach everyone this dialect. Adults who did not speak it took evening classes. Today, all schoolchildren learn their lessons in Mandarin. National newscasts and television programs use this common language as well.

(above) Chinese schoolchildren practice their calligraphy using a brush dipped in ink.

Words as pictures

Chinese writing is different from the print in this book because it does not use an alphabet of letters. Chinese characters, or **pictographs**, represent whole words instead of letters or sounds. Each pictograph is like a picture that stands for an object or idea. There are over 50,000 symbols, but the average educated person knows only 8,000. Can you imagine having to learn 1,000 characters in order to read a simple book?

The communication age

Many types of media transmit information in China. There are over 2,000 newspapers, 4,000 magazines, and 200 radio stations across the country. Television is quickly becoming the most important news source in the nation. There are over thirty-five million television sets in China.

Computerized China

Computers have become important tools for communication. Many people use the Internet for work and leisure. Internet cafes are popular places to browse the World Wide Web and chat with people all over the world. The government requires that web surfers provide records of the information they obtain from the Internet as well as the people whom they contact through e-mail.

Information walls

With over a billion people in China, spreading information is a difficult task. The Chinese have a clever system for passing on important news. Public notice boards, called *dazibao*, are a common sight on streets and in factories. National newspapers, local announcements, and public education bulletins are tacked up on these boards. Anybody who has a message can pin it up for everyone to read.

(above) Computers in China use a simplified form of Mandarin.

(below) Newspapers are only one way that Chinese citizens learn about current events in their country.

School days

In the days when emperors ruled China, few people had the privilege of attending school. Only boys from the ruling class and a small number of peasants learned how to read and write. With the four treasures of study—ink, inkstones, paper, and brushes—these lucky students learned the teachings of the wise man Confucius.

Today, every child goes to school. Students attend school every day except Sunday. In some schools, Friday is excursion day and Saturday is spent in a park. Chinese children enjoy four weeks of holidays in the winter and six to eight weeks in the summer. Starting at age six, children attend school for at least nine years. After six years of primary school, students enter middle school for another three to six years. After three years of middle school, students can move on to schools that teach various technical job skills. After six years of middle school, students at the top of their classes can go on to university to become professionals such as doctors, engineers, scientists, agricultural specialists, and teachers.

Jump, twist, turn

In China the school day begins with ten minutes of exercise. Jumping, twisting, and turning makes everyone alert and ready to start classes as early as 8:00 a.m. At noon, children take a two-hour lunch break and then go back to class until 4:30 p.m. In both rural and city schools, children help clean their classrooms and school yards.

In the younger grades, students spend time mastering the difficult brushstrokes of Chinese writing and the ancient skill of using the **abacus**. An abacus is a hand-operated computing device using beads as counters. Students use it instead of a calculator to solve math problems.

(below) This kindergarten class starts the day with fresh air and exercise!

After-school fun

Most Chinese students do not go straight home after their classes are done. Instead, they go to recreation centers called "Children's Palaces." Here, children enjoy many different activities including drawing, clay modeling, and dancing. Children who are especially good at one activity, such as gymnastics, receive extra training.

Rural education

For a long time, few villages had schools. Rural families needed children to work on the farms, so many of these children did not attend classes. Even today, many village schools are small and poorly equipped. Sometimes the floors are made of earth, and several grades are taught together by one teacher. In some areas, children have to walk for over an hour to reach the nearest school.

Better education

In the past few years, many new schools have been built in small villages. The government is making a great effort to educate everyone, including the people in the most remote areas.

(above) At a Children's Palace in Shanghai, students practice ballet.

(below) These students attend Middle School in Beijing.

Making a living

Business is booming in China! Never before have the Chinese people known such prosperity. New businesses such as street cafes, luxury hotels, and factories of all kinds have opened everywhere. Large billboards advertise modern appliances for sale at fancy, air-conditioned department stores.

New policies

When the **communist** government came into power in 1949, China was a poverty-stricken, war-torn land. The government took control of production and trade so everyone would have food, shelter, and a job. In 1979, China introduced two new plans—the open policy and the responsibility system. The open policy has enabled China to welcome foreigners into the country and trade goods with other countries . Many coastal towns and cities as well as Hong Kong have been named Special Economic Zones. In these areas foreign companies and investors can **invest** in Chinese businesses. Many form joint ventures, or businesses owned by both Chinese and foreign companies.

The responsibility system allows people to make extra money. Previously, people were paid the same wage no matter how hard they worked. As a result, the economy did not prosper. Now, Chinese citizens are allowed to start their own small businesses. With the extra money people earn, they are able to buy factory-made goods such as bicycles, sewing machines, and electronic products.

Private farming

More than half of China's population still makes a living off the land. At one time, people worked on farming **communes** where up to 20,000 people worked together. Now, these farms have been divided into smaller units, and family work groups and village communities are in charge of their own production. Families manage private plots as well. Farmers give a portion of their crops to the government and sell the rest in free markets, which are not government-controlled. At free markets, goods are sold at competitive prices instead of at prices set by the government.

Assigned jobs

In the past, the government assigned people jobs on farms or in factories. Although the pay was low, workers received many benefits, such as medical care, education, day care, and housing. Some people still work for companies, such as hydroelectric plants and steel factories, that are owned and operated by the government. These companies are known as state-owned enterprises.

New choices

Chinese workers have more choices than ever before. People are allowed to choose their own careers instead of being assigned to positions when they finish school or training. Some people find a job on their own or with the help of a job-placement agency. Others open their own businesses. Universities are training more and more students to become doctors, engineers, teachers, and technology experts. These new opportunities have encouraged people to work harder for both themselves and their country.

(opposite) More and more executives can be seen in western-style business suits.

(right and below) These workers are employed in a shoe and a glove factory.

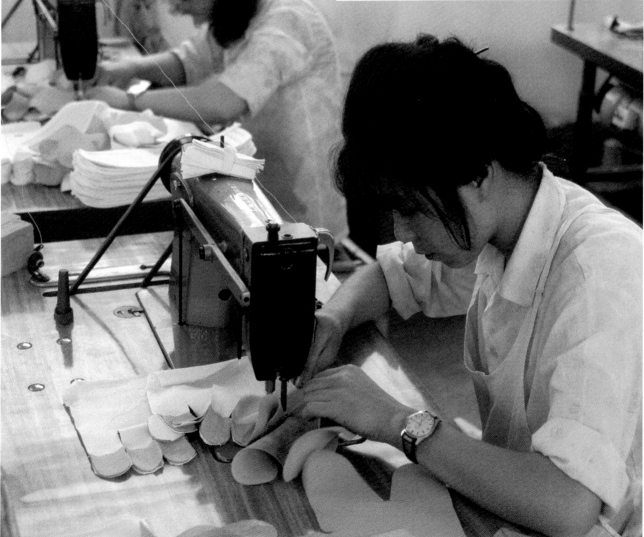

Private business

For over twenty years, the Chinese government has been encouraging people to make money on their own. Millions of people have become involved in private businesses of one kind or another. Business owners range from pig farmers and flower sellers to restaurant owners and dentists. Many businesses start on the street. If the businesses prosper, street vendors sometimes rent stores and set up permanent shops.

Cottage industries are businesses that are conducted in people's homes. Some early cottage industries have grown into huge factories that now employ many people. For example, a local artisan skilled in making ceramics may open a small shop operated from his or her home. As the business grows, the artist begins to train helpers. Today, there are thousands of privately owned factories that produce everything from fine leather shoes to bubble gum.

From public to private

Private businesses often make more money than state-owned enterprises, even though private business owners pay high taxes. Many state-owned enterprises are losing money and are being sold to private owners. When state-owned enterprises are sold, many workers lose their jobs.

(left) A woman buys fresh fish at a market.

(below) A local tailor prepares his material.

(above) A barber makes a living right on the street.

(left) A tradesman weighs some eels for a sale.

(below) A couple sells spices at the market.

Leisure and sports

Chinese people today have more free time than ever before, so they are participating in a wide range of leisure activities. City residents learn traditional arts and crafts at community centers or "Cultural Palaces." Country dwellers make their own fun. They play games such as cards and Chinese chess.

Outdoor fun

Because of crowded conditions, Chinese people live in small homes that do not have room for entertaining. As a result, they spend much of their free time outside. On summer evenings, neighbors gather together in courtyards to play cards or chess. On Sundays, many families visit historic sites such as the Great Wall or enjoy a rowboat ride in a park. Other favorite activities are gardening, shopping, and visiting with friends at local restaurants and outdoor cafes.

Parks and songbirds

Parks are used by people of all ages, but they are especially popular among the elderly. In China, men retire at age sixty and women at age fifty. In order to keep active after retirement they take up a number of hobbies. A favorite pastime is training songbirds. These birds are kept in delicate bamboo cages. Their owners take them for walks to nearby parks where they hang their cages from trees. The birds relish the fresh air, and the owners enjoy admiring one another's pets.

Sports

Sports are popular with people of all ages. Ping-pong, basketball, volleyball, swimming, gymnastics, and shadow boxing are all favorites. Most Chinese people participate in some kind of physical activity.

Ping-pong

Ping-pong may be considered the national sport of China because so many people play it. In winter, it is played indoors; in summer, it becomes an outdoor game. Outdoors, temporary tables are constructed by placing a table top on bricks or concrete blocks. Even the net is made out of a row of bricks! People play ping-pong just about everywhere—in parks, courtyards, sports centers, and school yards.

Martial arts

For centuries, the people of China have practiced martial arts. They were once used in combat against enemies. Today, they are studied and practiced by millions of people. Some martial arts are associated with religion, such as the *shao lin* boxing exercises. *Shao lin* was developed to help monks stay awake during long meditation sessions.

Tai chi chuan

At dawn, hundreds of people, including many elderly, dress in loose clothing and gather in parks or other open spaces to practice the graceful exercises of *tai chi chuan*. *Tai chi chuan* is a series of 128 body movements. The purpose of these movements is to keep the body in constant motion without losing balance or breaking concentration.

This gentle form of exercise developed from a belief system called **Taoism**. Participants focus their energy and thoughts on moving smoothly and gracefully. Practicing *tai chi chuan* is harder than it looks! The exercises demand great muscle control. It is important to relax one's mind and control one's breathing. Most of the basic positions are named after animals such as the eagle, bear, horse, cat, dog, snake, and leopard. Some of the movements are so beautiful that they are also used on stage in Chinese operas.

(opposite, bottom) Parks provide space for games and other activities. Young people practice ping-pong in the park.

(above) These men are enjoying a game of Chinese checkers in a park.

(right) An acrobat performs on the street for an enthusiastic crowd.

Glossary

abacus An ancient counting machine using rows of beads on a wooden frame

ancestors People from whom one is descended

autonomous Free from outside control; independent

Buddhism A religion founded on Buddha, an ancient religious leader from India

civilization A society with a well-established culture that has existed for a long period of time

communism An economic system in which the country's resources are held in common by all the people and regulated by the government

commune A community in which land is held in common, and where members live and work together

Confucius An ancient Chinese scholar whose ideas have greatly influenced Chinese society

culture The customs, beliefs, and arts of a group of people

dazibao The Chinese word for information walls where important news is posted

dialect A variation of a language

extended family A family unit including grandparents, aunts, uncles, and cousins

folk religion The informal beliefs of the common people of an area

generation People born at about the same time. Grandparents, parents, and children make up three generations.

industrialized A term used to describe a society that produces manufactured goods in factories

Islam A religion based on the teachings of Muhammed. Its followers are called Muslims.

Lama Buddhism A religion that combines the teachings of Buddha and the Dalai Lama, the spiritual leader of Tibet

manual work Work that is done by hand rather than by machine

martial art A sport that uses fighting techniques and self-defense moves

minority A small group that differs from the larger group of which it is a part

modern conveniences Up-to-date goods and services that make life easier, such as electricity and running water

national group People who share a common background and lifestyle

nomads People who wander from place to place in search of food or land on which their animals can graze

oasis An area of a desert that is kept fertile by underground springs

ornament A small, brightly-colored object used for decoration

pictograph A picture used to represent a word

plateau An area of flat land raised above the surrounding land

protest A public declaration of a complaint or disagreement, often done by a group of people

putonghua The Mandarin dialect, now the national language of China

rural Relating to the countryside

sampan A small boat with one sail and a flat bottom, often used as a houseboat

sanitary conditions Conditions that promote better health, such as cleanliness and proper sewage disposal

Taoism A religion based on the teachings of Laotzu, an ancient Chinese philosopher

yurt A portable dome-shaped tent made of many layers of felt laid over a wooden frame

Index

1 2 3 4 5 6 7 8 9 0 Printed in the USA 5 4 3 2 1 0